National Audit Office

Cross-government

Conflicts of interest

Report by the Comptroller and Auditor General

Ordered by the House of Commons
to be printed on 26 January 2015

This report has been prepared under Section 6 of the National Audit Act 1983 for presentation to the House of Commons in accordance with Section 9 of the Act

Sir Amyas Morse KCB
Comptroller and Auditor General
National Audit Office

23 January 2015

HC 907 | £10.00

This report provides an overview of what conflicts of interest are, the risks and how and why they occur and includes various examples from public sector situations

10542 01/15 NAO

Contents

The National Audit Office study team consisted of:
Ee-Ling Then, Simon Reason, under the direction of Paul Oliffe.

This report can be found on the National Audit Office website at www.nao.org.uk

For further information about the National Audit Office please contact:

National Audit Office
Press Office
157–197 Buckingham Palace Road
Victoria
London
SW1W 9SP

Tel: 020 7798 7400

Enquiries: www.nao.org.uk/contact-us

Website: www.nao.org.uk

Twitter: @NAOorguk

Summary

1 This report outlines the importance of recognising and adequately managing conflicts of interest in the public sector. We define a conflict of interest as a set of circumstances that creates a risk that an individual's ability to apply judgement or act in one role is, or could be, impaired or influenced by a secondary interest. The perception of competing interests, impaired judgement or undue influence can also be a conflict of interest.

2 In the last year we have gathered a significant amount of intelligence on conflicts, particularly in the health and education sectors. These are areas of government where services are increasingly commissioned and delivered by parties at arm's-length to departments.

3 Conflicts of interest can occur naturally as a product of the way a system is designed. Providing services via third parties increases the potential for conflicts of interest as organisations act as both commissioner and provider of related services. A clear approach to managing these conflicts is necessary to counter concerns about lack of transparency and the view that conflicts of interest are influencing decisions. A particular concern alleges that commissioners have been able to buy services from private businesses in which they have a financial or family interest.

4 It is important to recognise the risk of conflicts of interest and their impact on how decisions and operations are perceived. A failure to recognise a conflict of interest can give the impression that the organisation or individual is not acting in the public interest and could potentially lead to a decision being subject to challenge. This can damage reputations and undermine confidence in government.

5 This report gives examples of potential conflicts to illustrate how and where they may arise in the provision of public services. Our objectives were to:

- define conflicts of interest (Part One);
- explain how and where conflicts of interest can arise and the importance of recognising them when they do occur (Part Two); and
- determine what guidance and policies govern the management of conflicts of interest and establish what should be in place to identify and manage the risks (Part Three).

6 This report uses examples of potential conflicts as illustrations. We have not sought to judge whether an actual conflict of interest has arisen and/or influenced decision-making. We also did not assess government or departmental conflict of interest policies or practices in this report. We plan to focus on how conflicts of interest are managed in specific sectors seperately in planned future work.

7 Our methods are set out at Appendix One. We summarise key elements of good practice on managing conflicts of interest in Appendix Two.

Part One

Defining conflicts of interest

What are conflicts of interest?

1.1 A conflict of interest is a set of circumstances that creates a risk that an individual's ability to apply judgement or act in one role is, or could be, impaired or influenced by a secondary interest. It can occur in any situation where an individual or organisation (private or government) can exploit a professional or official role for personal or other benefit. This definition is based on generally accepted standards.

1.2 Conflicts can exist if the circumstances create a risk that decisions *may* be influenced, regardless of whether the individual actually benefits. The perception of competing interests, impaired judgement or undue influence can also be a conflict of interest.

1.3 Conflicts might occur if individuals have, for example:

- a direct or indirect financial interest;
- non-financial or personal interests; or
- conflicts of loyalty where decision-makers have competing loyalties between an organisation they owe a primary duty to and some other person or entity.

1.4 Conflicts of interest exist on a spectrum of severity. In public services, they can take many forms, for example:

- accepting hospitality or gifts from private sector companies during a procurement exercise;
- providing policy advice to government while also working or consulting, for industry;
- awarding contracts to suppliers in which the decision-maker has a personal or financial interest; and
- in the delivery of public services, where individuals or organisations assess service needs as well as providing the services.

Consequences of not recognising the risk of conflicts

1.5 It is important to manage conflicts of interest. Not only can they bring decision-making into disrepute but often the perception of conflict alone is enough to cause concern. This can lead to reputational damage and undermine public confidence in the integrity of institutions.

1.6 A failure to recognise a conflict of interest can give the impression that the organisation or individual is not acting in the public interest. More seriously, if left unresolved, some conflicts can result in criminal action, for example fraud, bribery or corruption through abuse of position.

1.7 There is also a potential risk of legal challenge to decisions made by public bodies. If a decision-maker has a conflict of interest then the decision is potentially vulnerable and could be overturned on judicial review.[1]

1 Article 6 of the European Convention on Human Rights and Articles 41 and 47 of the EU Charter of Fundamental Rights enshrine the principle that decisions should be made free from actual and apparent bias.

Part Two

Recognising the risk of conflicts of interest

2.1 This part of the report describes why it is important to recognise conflicts. It also provides examples of where they commonly arise.

2.2 Conflicts of interest are a common and unavoidable part of management that can arise in a range of situations and environments. They can result from policy decisions or systems or can occur naturally in certain management situations. It is therefore not reasonable or desirable to completely eliminate the risk of conflicts of interest. It is better to recognise the associated risks and put measures in place to identify and manage conflicts when they do arise. Departments and other bodies should design a proportionate approach that reflects the nature and scale of conflicts that they are exposed to and their risk appetite (**Figure 1**).

2.3 The following sections describe the types of situations where conflicts are more likely to occur. We use case examples to illustrate our points not to form a judgement. At times, the examples highlight allegations reported by the media. We use such examples to show how conflicts are perceived, not with the intent of supporting the allegations or commenting on whether the conflicts were appropriately managed.

Figure 1
Taking a proportionate approach to managing conflicts

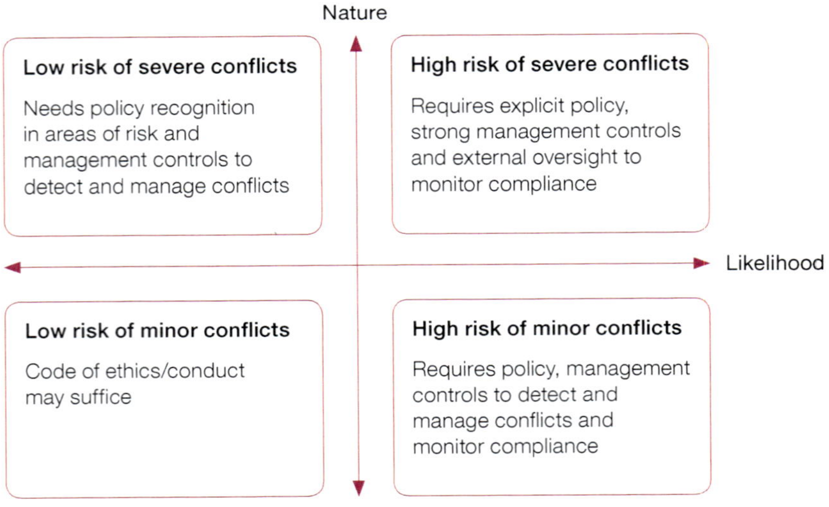

Source: National Audit Office

Conflicts arising from the design of policy/system

2.4 Conflicts of interest can arise from system or policy design. Changes in public service provision have created devolved delivery models. Private or semi-private organisations assess service needs and then, either directly or indirectly, provide the service. For example, GPs could be both commissioners and providers of services for clinical commissioning groups. They are responsible for selecting providers and deciding on spending, while potentially being involved in delivering some of those services.

2.5 Academy trusts and local enterprise partnerships are in a similar position. Members of such groups come from different backgrounds, bringing valuable local, specialist or business expertise. However, there are allegations surrounding the lack of transparency in decision-making and the risk that the private interests of members could influence public spending decisions, for example through related party transactions.

2.6 Related party transactions are a type of conflict of interest. The accounting standards define them as "a transfer of resources, services or obligations between a reporting entity and a related party, regardless of whether a price is charged".[2] Most commonly, they take the form of buying goods or services from companies in which the organisation – or individuals within that organisation – has some relationship with. They are not inherently irregular and are permitted.

Related party transactions in government

Health

2.7 When the Department of Health planned the reform of the health system in England which occurred in April 2013, it recognised the proposals increased the likelihood of conflicts of interest. But it felt the benefits outweighed the risks, so the Health and Social Care Act 2012 explicitly outlines how to manage conflicts.[3] The design of the reformed system means there is the potential for some GPs to profit personally from the decisions of commissioners, for example by commissioning services from a provider to which they have links.

2.8 A *British Medical Journal* investigation in 2013 found that 426 (36%) of the 1,179 GPs on the governing body of new clinical commissioning groups have a potential conflict of interest because they have directorships or shares in private healthcare companies.[4] These figures are not a cause for concern as long as each group identifies and manages these conflicts appropriately. We plan to produce a separate report on this area in 2015.

2 International Accounting Standard 24 on related party disclosures.

3 See Health and Social Care Act 2012, Chapter 2, Section 14O, available at: www.legislation.gov.uk/ukpga/2012/7/part/1/crossheading/further-provision-about-clinical-commissioning-groups/enacted

4 G Iacobucci, '*BMJ investigation finds GP conflicts of interest "rife" on commissioning boards*', *BMJ* 12 March 2013, available at: www.bmj.com/press-releases/2013/03/12/bmj-investigation-finds-gp-conflicts-interest-%E2%80%9Crife%E2%80%9D-commissioning-boards

Education

2.9 Academies is another sector where conflicts occur and in some cases, they have not been appropriately managed. Academy trusts are charitable companies limited by guarantee, so must comply with relevant charities and companies law. This legislation includes the requirement that trustees act in the trust's interest, and disclose all related party transactions in its annual report and accounts. Academies must also comply with the *Academies financial handbook*. This guidance previously prohibited trustees from 'benefiting personally' from their relationship with a trust. However, the new guidance for the year ended 31 August 2014 says all related party transactions should be 'at cost', without any profit element.

2.10 The Department for Education and the Education Funding Agency oversee the academies sector. The Agency requires transparent self-declaration of related-party transactions in academies' audited and published accounts. It also investigates shortcomings in performance, publishing its investigations to promote openness.[5] In a recent review, it found that in a small number of cases, conflicts of interest were not managed appropriately.[6] Academy trusts or individuals were in breach of the guidelines, sometimes leading to a *Financial Notice to Improve* or even to criminal proceedings. We have examined the Education Funding Agency's wider management controls on related party transactions but have not undertaken a systematic review to quantify the scale of the issue.[7]

2.11 This report provides illustrative examples drawn from the published education investigations. The number of examples in this report should not be taken to demonstrate greater issues in this sector relative to others. There is more information available on education due to the Department and Agency's efforts to examine this issue in more detail.

2.12 Cases show schools awarding contracts to private businesses in which their staff, trustees, governors or sponsors had a financial interest. Potentially these give trustees or their families opportunities to profit from their relationship with the academy or school trust. There are examples where:

- trusts awarded contracts for services to companies in which certain members of the trust had an interest;
- members failed to declare their interests when taking the decisions to award the contracts in question; and
- sponsors provided paid services through licensing arrangements.

5 Education Funding Agency, *Academies investigation reports*, 7 March 2014, available at: www.gov.uk/government/collections/academies-investigation-reports

6 Education Funding Agency, *Review of related party transactions in academies,* November 2014, available at: www.gov.uk/government/publications/review-of-related-party-transactions-in-academies

7 Comptroller and Auditor General, *Investigation into the Education Funding Agency's oversight of related party transactions at Durand Academy*, Session 2014-15, HC 782, National Audit Office, November 2014.

2.13 The Institute for Education published research in September 2014 into conflicts of interest in academy sponsorship arrangements. The research was small-scale and rapid. It noted that:

> "The widespread view, is that the majority of academy trusts are staffed by honourable people working hard to address educational underperformance, often in challenging circumstances. Cases of deliberate fraud are rare and many of the instances where real or perceived conflicts have arisen are the result of people being asked to work too fast with too few controls. Nevertheless, the general sense… is that the checks and balances on academy trusts in relation to conflicts of interest are still too weak. In the course of the research we came across a significant number of real or potential conflicts of interest that we found concerning."
>
> *Source: Professor Toby Greany and Jean Scott, Conflicts of interest in academy sponsorship arrangements: A report for the Education Select Committee, London Centre for Leadership Learning and Institute of Education, September 2014*

Local government

2.14 Local Enterprise Partnerships are another area of potential risk. These were established in 2011 as voluntary partnerships between local authorities and businesses to help lead economic growth and job creation. They decide what the local priorities should be for investment in roads, buildings and facilities in defined areas. Members are drawn from the public and private sector, with the chair coming from business. There has been some media attention questioning the impartiality of funding decisions given the risk that some members have business interests and could benefit personally, for example in planning applications.[8] However, we have not yet looked at this and therefore cannot comment on the extent to which there is an issue. The government has developed an assurance framework which sets out how conflicts of interest should be dealt with.[9]

Conflicts arising from operational situations

2.15 Conflicts of interest are more likely to arise where individuals or organisations are transacting with a third party. This includes commissioning and procurement decisions; recruiting staff; leaving public office; partnering with private firms; and when receiving gifts. Organisations should manage this risk by putting in place appropriate safeguards around these operations.

8 Media articles, available at: www.bournemouthecho.co.uk/news/11241945.LEP_member_accused_of____staggering_conflict_of_interest____after_supporting_Winter_Gardens_scheme/, www.coventrytelegraph.net/news/coventry-news/call-block-bizarre-coventry-warwickshire-3022034 and www.bbc.co.uk/news/uk-england-coventry-warwickshire-18718966

9 Department for Business, Innovation & Skills, *Local enterprise partnership assurance framework*, December 2014, available at: www.gov.uk/government/uploads/system/uploads/attachment_data/file/386642/bis-14-1241-local-enterprise-partnership-LEP-national-assurance-framework.pdf

Commissioning and procurement decisions

2.16 Public procurement is vulnerable to conflicts of interest. Selecting a contractor to provide supplies or services provides opportunities for conflicts as personal and professional connections can influence choice. For example, someone could influence the tender procedure to allow a relative, friend or commercial or financial partner to increase their chances of success. They could leak information on the tendering procedure, bias the selection criteria or influence the final evaluation. **Figure 2** gives an example of a public official awarding a contract for personal gain.

Recruitment and selection of staff

2.17 Recruiting and selecting staff is open to the same risks as selecting suppliers. There needs to be transparent processes and criteria to ensure decisions are made objectively and without bias. **Figure 3** describes an example of nepotism in an academy.

Additional employment, outside appointments and activity after leaving public office

2.18 Individuals transferring from government to private sector roles are associated with many apparent conflicts of interest, for example:

- Abuse of office: an official might use his or her power while in office to shape a policy or decision in favour of a certain company, with a view to opening up opportunities to future employment.
- Undue influence: a former officer now employed by a private company might influence his or her former colleagues to make a decision that favours the company.
- Profiteering: an individual might profit from public office by drawing on information, knowledge or stature derived from his or her public role to profit financially.
- Switching sides: an individual might leave public office to take up employment with a private sector organisation in a role that requires him or her to oppose the government's position on an issue, which he or she had previously represented. This can be problematic because they may have had access to privileged information.[10]

10 Taken from Transparency International UK, *Corruption in UK local government, the mounting risks*, October 2013, pp. 26–27.

Figure 2
Procurement practices

Revenue & Customs Prosecutions Office (example from NAO financial audit)

In 2005-06, the Comptroller and Auditor General qualified the accounts of the Revenue and Customs Procurement Office and highlighted procurement irregularities. The chief operating officer had engaged his wife to do a human resource review in 2005-06. In 2006-07, he made payments to a company owned by his wife of which he was the company secretary. Payments over 2 years totalled £97,907 (including VAT). There were no clear procurement controls (including inadequate separation of duties), no code of conduct and the organisation failed to alert HM Treasury before the transaction. It was also not disclosed as a related party transaction.

Source: Revenue and Customs Prosecutions Office Resource Account 2006-07; Select committee on public accounts, Memorandum by the Comptroller and Auditor General updating his reports HC 273 of 2005-06 and HC 870 of 2006-07, May 2008

Figure 3
Recruiting family members

Priory Federation of Academies (example from Department for Education investigation)

An investigation into the Federation found a history of employing relatives of staff. The former chief executive officer (CEO) employed his wife at the federation, and also his daughter, son and the former finance director's son.

The CEO's daughter was engaged as a consultant from May 2010 to April 2011 at a cost of £55,585. This figure was not declared in the 31 August 2011 accounts as a third party transaction. The investigators were told it was not clear from guidance what constitutes a 'close relative' – the trigger for a declaration. His son was employed for 5 months from February 2011 and paid around £19,000. His wife was paid £6,030 in October 2008 for consultancy.

The CEO resigned and was subject to police investigation in 2012-13.

Source: Department for Education. Internal Audit, *Investigation Report on Priory Federation of Academies Trust*, March 2012. Available at: http://media.education.gov.uk/assets/files/pdf/d/priory%20federation%20of%20academies%20trust%20dfe%20investigation%20report%20march%202012.pdf

2.19 There are business appointment rules which apply to civil servants who intend to take up an appointment or employment after leaving the Civil Service. Senior civil servants may need to seek approval from the Advisory Committee on Business Appointments who can impose certain conditions such as a waiting period and/or a prohibition on the individual being involved in lobbying government on behalf of their new employer. Other restrictions could include a condition that for a specified period, the former civil servant should stand aside from involvement in certain activities, for example, commercial dealings with his or her former Department, or involvement in particular areas of the new employer's business. The advice for the most senior civil servants is usually made public once the appointment is announced or taken up. Recent changes to the rules also now require Departments to publish summary information on the advice and restrictions imposed on their former civil servants below this senior level.[11]

11 Cabinet Office, *the business appointment rules for civil servants*, available at: www.gov.uk/government/uploads/system/uploads/attachment_data/file/382937/Business_Appointment_Rules__2014_.pdf

2.20 Figure 4 gives 2 examples, reported in the media.

Contracted-out services

2.21 The private sector is increasingly involved in providing a range of public services including directly delivering front-line services. As a result, employees of private companies can be expected to make important decisions about the delivery of services on the government's behalf. However, for a private company, balancing delivering value to the public with maximising returns to shareholders can sometimes lead to conflicts.

Figure 4
Movement of staff between government and private companies

Procurement of search and rescue helicopters (example from open source media)

In 2011, the Ministry of Defence (MoD) and Department for Transport (DfT) terminated their procurement of new search and rescue helicopters. The preferred bidder in the competition, a consortium, had come forward to inform them that there were irregularities in their bid team. Specifically the consortium had gained access to commercially sensitive information regarding the joint MoD/DfT evaluations of industry bids.

In 2013, an investigation by the Ministry of Defence police found there was insufficient evidence to warrant further police action. At the time of our fieldwork the Department in partnership with the MoD was pursuing a civil claim.[1]

From designing policy to private delivery (example from open source media)

The BBC reported on the case of a former director general of commissioning at the Department of Health, who in 2009, 3 months after leaving his position, became Global Head of Health care at KPMG. Having been responsible for designing ways of commissioning healthcare, the individual then worked for a company that was bidding for many of the contracts resulting from his reforms.

The individual sought advice on his career move from the Advisory Committee on Business Appointments (ACoBA), as he was required to do. The appointment had been approved subject to a 3-month waiting period and a 12-month ban on lobbying ministers. His successor at the Department of Health also joined KPMG a year later. He did not have to seek ACoBA approval as he had only served as 'acting' Director General of Commissioning. However, the Department gave its approval and imposed the same conditions on him.[2] KPMG went on to win 3 NHS related contracts.

KPMG stated that "both men had actively observed and fully complied at all times with the restrictions placed on them... KPMG has ensured that neither was involved in contract bids which would have been in conflict with those restrictions. KPMG requires all new joiners to sign a confirmation that they will comply with specific requirements to act with integrity and ensure that conflicts of interest do not occur. These contracts have been awarded via competitive tenders under formal public sector procurement processes."

Notes

1 Hansard, Parliamentary question by Sir Alan Beith, HC Deb, 25 April 2013, c1266W.

2 This case was reported by BBC Radio 4's File on 4 programme, broadcast on 26 July 2011 (programme number: 11VQ5007LHO). Transcript available at: http://news.bbc.co.uk/1/shared/bsp/hi/pdfs/fileon4_26_07_11_revolve.pdf It was quoted in a Transparency International UK policy paper: *Fixing the revolving door between government and business*, May 2012.

Source: See notes

2.22 Departments who decide to contract out their services should identify any potential conflicts of interest that its contractors may have, and ensure they and their contractors have appropriate means to manage them. Our recent report *Transforming government's contract management* sets out the need for the contractor to take greater responsibility for providing a control environment which will maintain ethical behaviour and public service standards. The report also suggests that government ask its contractors to provide annual statements of assurance that they have operated appropriate controls.[12] **Figure 5** describes an example of how conflicts are being managed in a contracted-out service.

Figure 5
Handling dual roles

Supplying temporary workers to government (example from open source media)

In June 2013, The Crown Commercial Service (CCS) introduced the 'Contingent Labour One' contract to provide temporary resources into central government and arm's-length bodies. All temporary posts are now sourced by one of three suppliers: Capita Business Services; Hays Plc; and Brook Street. These suppliers contract with employment agencies who, in turn, recruit temporary contractors to fill posts. These suppliers or their parent companies also own employment agencies directly.

Capita Business Services provides a service to source specialist contractors and interim managers from a supply chain of some 290 agencies. The supply chain is managed by Capita Business Services and all suppliers are vetted and approved for use in the contract. Suppliers can submit up to 2 candidate CVs per advertised role that are then reviewed and sifted by Capita Business Services. It then provides the 5 most appropriate CVs to the employer (department or arm's-length body) to select. The successful supplier then receives a fixed mark-up of the day rate as a commission.

Press reports have focused on how Capita Business Services faces a conflict of interest as there are businesses in the Capita Group which are employment agencies and can supply contractors as well as being the service provider. The CCS manages it by:

- requiring the Capita Group employment agencies to compete with other employment agencies when a new role is advertised;
- including a contractual clause that caps the total value of work Capita Group employment agencies can provide to a maximum of 20% over a six month period – at least 80% of vacancies by value must be fulfilled by non-Capita Group employment agencies; and
- monitoring performance against this by requiring Capita Business Servies to report monthly information on the source of candidates for the value of contracts won. Capita Group cannot submit candidates from its own employment agencies if the cap is breached without CCS's prior permission.

The 20% cap was put in place following CCS costing research. This found that it would be prohibitively expensive for a supplier to administer the system without the ability to compete for roles through the employment agencies within its own group. CCS therefore decided to allow the supplier to compete with the supply chain to provide contractors up to a specified threshold.

Brook Street provides a managed service for the provision of administrative and clerical roles and Hays plc for operational roles. Due to the lower costs associated with these types of roles, both Hays plc and Brook Street can provide their own candidates for up to 80% of the work by value.

Source: Crown Commercial Service

12 Comptroller and Auditor General, *Transforming government's contract management*, Session 2014-15, HC 269, National Audit Office, September 2014, paragraph 3.17.

Gifts and hospitality

2.23 Accepting significant gifts or hospitality creates a perception of biased decision-making even if the gift has no bearing on judgement. The Bribery Act 2010 defines bribery as offering or receiving a bribe in return for breach of expectation or improper performance and sets out 4 criminal offences: bribing another person; being bribed; bribery of a foreign public official; and failure of a commercial organisation to prevent a bribe. Under Section 7, commercial organisations need to show they have 'adequate procedures' in place to prevent persons associated with them from undertaking such conduct.

2.24 The legislation does not criminalise corporate hospitality or other expenditure which is reasonable and proportionate. It is accepted that this is a recognised and established part of doing business. But in some instances it may be perceived that the real purpose behind the expenditure is to influence an individual in order to secure business or a business advantage.

2.25 The civil service code states that "civil servants must not receive gifts, hospitality or benefits of any kind from a third party which might be seen to compromise their personal judgement or integrity." We expect departments should have arrangements in place to declare and register gifts and other benefits. However, they decide the situations in which they require staff to report offers of gifts, hospitality and other benefits and the circumstances in which they need to seek permission before accepting them.[13]

2.26 Transparency is an important part of holding individuals to account for their actions. Since 2010, government has required departments to publish online, information about hospitatlity, gifts, travel and meetings with external organisations for ministers, the most senior officials and special advisors.[14] The latest data relates to 2013-14.

13 Available at: www.gov.uk/government/publications/civil-servants-terms-and-conditions
14 Available at: www.parliament.uk/business/committees/committees-archive/public-administration-select-committee/pasclobbying/

Part Three

Managing conflicts of interest

3.1 This part of the report describes the UK's approach to reducing the risk of conflicts arising and the practical measures public sector organisations should have in place to manage conflicts of interest.

How to manage conflicts of interest

3.2 Countries opt to 'regulate' conflicts of interest in different ways, reflecting historical, political and cultural circumstances. In most countries, preventing conflicts of interest is part of a broader policy to combat corruption. Approaches fall on a spectrum from an absolute, rules-based model to a more informal principles-based approach.

UK government approach to managing conflicts

3.3 The UK public sector takes a principles-based approach, indirectly addressing conflicts of interest through ethical standards and behaviour. There is high-level central government direction on how to manage conflicts of interest with guidance and codes of conduct to outline principles and expected behaviour for civil servants, board members and accounting officers. It relies on local implementation and enforcement:

- The Committee on Standards in Public Life's 'Nolan principles', and the *Civil Service code of conduct*, refer to 'integrity' and the need to put obligations of public service above personal interests.[15]
- The Cabinet Office's *Civil Service management code* sets out principles and rules for departments and agencies on terms and conditions of service – it includes sections on standards and propriety, including a requirement for civil servants to disclose business interests.[16]

15 Committee on Standards in public life, *the 7 principles of public life*, May 1995, available at: www.gov.uk/government/publications/the-7-principles-of-public-life; Cabinet Office, *Civil Service Code*, November 2010, available at: www.civilservice.gov.uk/wp-content/uploads/2011/09/civil-service-code-2010.pdf

16 The code states that civil servants should not be involved in any decision which could affect the value of their private investments, or the value of those on which they give advice to others, or use information acquired in the course of their work to advance their private financial interests or those of others. They must therefore declare to their department or agency any business interests which they or members of their immediate family could further as a result of their official position. They must comply with any subsequent instructions from their department regarding the retention, management or disposal of such interests. Cabinet Office, *Civil Service management code*, Section 4.3, October 2014, available at: www.gov.uk/government/publications/civil-servants-terms-and-conditions

- The Treasury's *Managing public money* outlines measures accounting officers and board members could take if they encounter a conflict[17] – its corporate governance code for good practice for departments mentions the need for board members to declare and record conflicts of interest but does not cover how these should be managed.[18]

3.4 Public sector organisations are expected to develop and set up their own approach under this central framework. Departments and agencies are responsible for defining the standards of conduct they require of their staff and for ensuring that these reflect the civil service management code and framework.[19] Departments are also responsible for enforcing compliance.

3.5 In contrast, the United States takes a rules-based approach where there are explicit, centrally-enforced requirements. **Figure 6** compares the approaches. For further information see the international reviews in the footnotes.[20]

Managing conflicts of interest in practice

3.6 As paragraph 3.4 notes, departments and agencies are responsible for putting in place arrangements to manage conflicts of interest. The way they decide to manage conflicts should reflect the risk of exposure to conflicts (discussed in Part Two). Those environments that are more prone to conflicts of interest need more management.

3.7 As a minimum, an organisation should have a system to identify and manage conflicts of interest rather than to eliminate them. The effect should be to make everyone aware of what to do if they suspect a conflict and ensure decision-making is efficient, transparent and fair. Rules should be clear and robust but not overly prescriptive or complex. This could be addressed explicitly in a 'conflicts of interest policy' or in other guidance covering risky areas such as procurement or HR. The policy should require staff and contractors to routinely declare all private, personal and financial interests relevant to:

- decision-making;
- management of contracts; and
- giving policy advice.

Usually this should be completed annually in addition to ad-hoc declarations as conflicts occur, such as during a procurement exercise. **Figure 7** describes an incident where interests were not declared.

17 HM Treasury, *Managing public money*, Sections 3.7, July 2013, available at: www.gov.uk/government/uploads/system/uploads/attachment_data/file/212123/Managing_Public_Money_AA_v2_-_chapters_annex_web.pdf

18 HM Treasury, *Corporate governance in central government departments: code of good practice*, July 2011, available at: www.gov.uk/government/publications/corporate-governance-code-for-central-government-departments

19 Cabinet Office, *Civil Service management code*, October 2014, available at: www.gov.uk/government/publications/civil-servants-terms-and-conditions

20 Sigma 2007, *Conflict of interest policies and practices in nine EU member states: a comparative review*, June 2007, available at: www.oecd.org/officialdocuments/publicdisplaydocumentpdf/?doclanguage=en&cote=gov/sigma(2006)1/REV1; OECD, *Managing conflicts of interest in the public sector, OECD guidelines and country experiences*, 2003; Transparency International, Anti-corruption Helpdesk, *Conflicts of interest in public procurement*, January 2013, available at: www.transparency.org/files/content/corruptionqas/Conflict_of_interest_in__public_procurement.pdf

Figure 6

The difference between a principles versus rules-based approach to managing conflicts of interest

	Principles-based approach eg UK	**Rules-based approach eg USA**[1]
Responsibility	Dispersed across government.	Office of Government Ethics.
Authority	No specific conflict of interest legislation. Local guidance. Companies Act applies to directors. Management code specifies some 'rules'.	Enforceable conflict of interest prohibitions defined in statute with criminal or civil penalties.
Other standards	Behavioural and ethical standards defined in codes of conduct and 'Nolan principles'.	Civil restrictions for certain outside activities. Administrative standards of conduct.
Disclosure requirements	Devolved, voluntary disclosure system for civil servants. MPs' financial interests are declared and published. Information on Senior civil servants and ministerial hospitality, gifts, travel and external meetings is published.	Central mandatory financial disclosure systems: • Public reporting is required for all senior officials. • Other employees make confidential financial disclosures.

Note

1 US Office of Government Ethics, available at: www.oge.gov/Topics/Financial-Conflicts-of-Interest-and-Impartiality/Financial-Conflicts-of-Interest---Impartiality/ and J S Ley, 'Managing conflicts of interest in the executive branch: the experience of the United States', in Organisation for Economic Cooperation and Development, *Managing Conflict in the Public Sector*, OECD guidelines and country experiences, pp. 231–249.

Source: National Audit Office research

Figure 7

Procurement in academies

Glendene Arts Academy (example from Department for Education investigation)

A contract for facilities management was awarded to a supplier under the 'Chair's emergency powers' without any justification. It appears that the Chair knew the owner of the company who was awarded the contract as both the Chair and owner were directors in another company. The Chair should have had no involvement in letting the contract, however he made no declarations of a conflict.

Source: Department for Education, Glendene Arts Academy investigation report, November 2013. Available at: www.gov.uk/government/uploads/system/uploads/attachment_data/file/296333/Investigation_report_Glendene_Arts_Academy.pdf

3.8 Where conflicts do arise, these should be clearly detailed, for example in the minutes of meetings, including a record of the action taken to manage the conflict. There should be clear rules on abstention and withdrawal from decision-making when participating places an individual in a conflicted position. If the conflict cannot be resolved in any other way, options could include divestment, recusal, transfer or restriction of activity. Some conflicts of interest may be so acute or pervasive that it would be better to avoid them entirely, for example the individual could resign. **Figure 8** illustrates where actions were taken to reduce possible conflicts of interest.

3.9 Departments and agencies should also have a code of ethics or code of conduct. Staff must confirm compliance with this regularly. The standards should define what behaviours and practices are acceptable and unacceptable and clearly state what will happen following non-compliance.

3.10 There is no explicit government guidance that applies to private and third sector bodies delivering services on their behalf.[21] However, there are provisions in company law for company directors.[22] Departments and agencies should share their policy, procedures or guidance so that providers are aware of their responsibilities and the consequences of non-compliance. Organisations can use formal contractual requirements to ensure standards and processes are understood.

Figure 8
Taking action to resolve a conflict

Decision-making in the Hillsborough review (example from open source media)

In 2013, the Director of Public Prosecutions (DPP), stood down from her supervisory role regarding the Hillsborough disaster prosecution. The appointment was criticised by campaign groups who said her involvement was inappropriate after it emerged that in 1996 she had provided advice to the Attorney General on the subject of a fresh inquest into the disaster.

Peter Lewis, chief executive officer of the Crown Prosecution Service, was appointed in her place. Although no conflict of interest was identified, he chose to recuse himself from decisions involving police conduct following the disaster, as he used to work as a prosecutor in the West Midlands. He remains overall decision-maker in respect of prosecution decisions with regards to the disaster itself but a colleague took over decisions related to police conduct following the disaster.

Source: R Pattinson, 'Second prosecutor steps down from Hillsborough role to avoid conflict of interest', Liverpool Echo, 20 October 2013, available at: www.liverpoolecho.co.uk/news/liverpool-news/hillsborough-conflict-interest-sees-crown-6212855

21 The Committee on Standards in Public Life, *Ethical standards for providers of public services*, June 2014.

22 Section 175 defines a duty for company directors to avoid situations in which they have, or could have, a direct or indirect interest that conflicts with, or might possibly conflict with, the interests of the company. Section 177 requires a director to disclose any interest, direct or indirect, that he has in relation to a proposed transaction or arrangement with the company. Section 182 requires a director to declare the nature and extent of any direct or indirect interest that he has in any transaction or arrangement entered into by the company.

Monitoring compliance

3.11 A system to manage conflicts of interest needs more than just policies, codes and declarations. A principles-based system assumes people will act honestly, and volunteer information about conflicts and exclude themselves from decision-making where conflicts exist. But there should be prompts and checks to reinforce this particularly where the risk of conflicts of interest is high. Preventative measures need to be supported by proportionate mechanisms to detect non-compliance and sanction where appropriate.

3.12 There should be management, internal controls and independent oversight to detect breaches of policy. Such controls may include:

- external oversight arrangements – for example, independent assurance that conflicts are appropriately managed and, arrangements for detecting breaches such as external audit and regulator checks; and
- a reporting system – such as whistleblowing arrangements for staff to raise concerns.[23]

3.13 In cases of non-compliance, there should be a system of proportionate, enforceable sanctions that include personal consequences (such as disciplinary action, dismissal or prosecution) and management actions (for example, retroactive cancellation of a decision or contract).

Independent checks

3.14 Independent checks are a way of dealing with conflicts and the perception of conflicts. **Figure 9** illustrates where a government programme introduced independent spot checks to strengthen oversight.

Figure 9
Strengthening compliance

Access to finance coaches (example from NAO review)

The Growth Accelerator Programme, run by the Department for Business, Innovation & Skills offers tailored support to help small businesses grow. One element of the programme is to improve access to finance via a coach who can suggest finance and investment options. The programme required coaches to declare any possible conflicts of interest as part of the selection process. However, once approved to deliver assignments, it relied on self-declaration to prevent conflicts of interest and did not prevent individual coaches encouraging clients to access finance or use investors the coach had a stake in. There were a small number of cases where investments were offered by an investor member of a brokerage or corporate finance company the coach was directly associated with.

The programme has since tightened up controls to minimise the risk of this happening. This includes banning introductory fees, requiring coaches to declare additional services recommended by clients, along with any benefit the coach would receive from those services and by monitoring the self-regulation by conducting spot checks of referrals.

Source: National Audit Office management letter to Department for Business, Innovation & Skills

23 Comptroller and Auditor General, *Making a whistleblowing policy work,* Session 2013-14, HC 1152, National Audit Office, March 2014. Available at: www.nao.org.uk/report/making-a-whistleblowing-policy-work

Appendix One

Our audit approach

Scope

1 This report examined policy and practice on managing conflicts of interest in public services. Our objectives were to:

- define conflicts of interest;
- determine what guidance and policies govern the management of conflicts of interest;
- provide examples of conflicts that have arisen in the delivery of public services, drawing on existing work and other intelligence; and
- establish a framework of what should be in place to identify and manage the consequences and risks of conflicts of interest.

Methods

2 In examining these issues, we primarily drew on **documentary review**.

3 We reviewed central policy and guidance to identify what guidelines and requirements exist on managing conflicts of interest in the public sector.

4 We reviewed a range of documents to identify examples of conflicts of interest, including:

- our back catalogue of financial audit, value for money and investigative work;
- investigative reports by other bodies, such as the Education Funding Agency; and
- media coverage on reported cases of conflicts of interest.

Appendix Two

Managing conflicts of interest – good practice

1 This summarises the key elements of good practice contained in the report, based on generally accepted standards.

Prevention

Promoting ethical standards (paragraph 3.9)

2 Departments and agencies should have a code of ethics or code of conduct. Staff must confirm compliance with this regularly.

3 These standards should define what behaviours and practices are acceptable and unacceptable. They should clearly state what will happen when people do not comply.

Identifying, understanding and managing conflicts of interest (paragraphs 3.6, 3.7 and 3.10)

4 There should be openness and transparency about situations where conflicts can and do arise. The intention should be to identify and manage conflicts of interest, not eliminate them. The effect should be to make everyone aware of what to do if they suspect a conflict and ensure decision-making is efficient, transparent and fair.

5 The way an organisation decide to manage conflicts should reflect the risk of exposure to conflicts. They should recognise the risk of conflicts of interest in policy, procedures or guidance, including what to do in cases where there is potential conflict of interest. This could be addressed explicitly in a 'conflicts of interest policy' or in other guidance covering risky areas such as procurement or HR. The procedures should comply with the law and good practice.

6 Departments and agencies should share their policy, procedures or guidance so that providers are aware of their responsibilities and the consequences of non-compliance. Organisations can use formal contractual requirements to ensure standards and processes are understood.

Transparency (paragraphs 2.25, 2.26)

7 Departments should have arrangements in place to declare and register gifts and other benefits.

Ensuring decisions are made independently (paragraphs 3.7, 3.8)

8 A policy should require staff and contractors to routinely declare all private, personal and financial interests relevant to:

- decision-making;
- management of contracts; and
- giving policy advice.

9 Usually this should be completed annually in addition to ad-hoc declarations as conflicts arise, such as during a procurement exercise.

10 Where conflicts do arise, these should be clearly detailed, for example in the minutes of meetings, including a record of the action taken to manage the conflict. There should be clear rules on abstention and withdrawal from decision-making when participating places an individual in a conflicted position. If the conflict cannot be resolved in any other way, options could include divestment, recusal, transfer, restriction of activity or resignation.

Detection and response (paragraphs 3.11 to 3.14)

11 A principles-based system assumes people will act honestly and volunteer information about conflicts and exclude themselves from decision-making where they exist. But there should also be prompts and checks to reinforce this particularly where the risk of conflicts of interest is high. Preventative measures need to be supported by proportionate mechanisms to detect non-compliance and sanction where appropriate.

12 There should be management, internal controls and independent oversight to detect breaches of policy. Such controls may include:

- external oversight arrangements – for example, independent assurance that conflicts are appropriately managed and arrangements for detecting breaches such as external audit and regulator checks; and
- a reporting system, such as whistleblowing arrangements for staff to raise concerns.

In cases of non-compliance, there should be a system of proportionate, enforceable sanctions that include personal consequences (such as disciplinary action, dismissal or prosecution) and management actions (for example, retroactive cancellation of a decision or contract).

Made in United States
Orlando, FL
04 November 2026

90208509R00017